After Difficulty…

Insights of W. Deen Mohammed

On

Pain and Suffering

Edited by Ronald B. Shaheed

Sincere thanks to Dr. Nasir Ahmad for diligently transcribing the material used to compile this book.

Edited and published by Ronald B. Shaheed

2015

Other books in the series:

Thoughts for Searchers Seeking to Understand Life

The Promised Human Destiny

ISBN: 978-0-692-39593-6

Photo on front cover taken by Ronald B. Shaheed

Foreword

Imam W. Deen Mohammed was one very familiar with physical pain and suffering. When he was a young adult he was thrown through the windshield of a car his brother was driving and sustained back injuries that plagued him for the rest of his life. Many years later he was diagnosed with type II diabetes and struggled with its challenges in the latter part of his life. In the midst of these and other bodily challenges he remained an energetic, erudite, and optimistic leader of his large following until his passing.

As the Qur'an, the holy book for Muslims, iterates, Imam W. Deen Mohammed believed that in everything there are signs, messages, or instructions, from *G_d. Consequently, he believed that in pain and suffering is a blessing. In this small publication we have attempted to share some of his direct thoughts on the blessings that come from difficulty, pain and suffering. We pray that the reader finds some benefit in these reflections.

The Editor

*In order to show due respect we do not, in this publication, use a spelling for the name of the Creator that can be seen as irreverent when read in reverse.

Contents

Introduction

Pain is the first part of G_d's Mercy. Pain itself is His mercy. When the doctor is giving you pain isn't it mercy? You say, "Oh doctor, it hurts!" But that's his mercy. You've got to do that to get the relief. Physical pain helps relieve mental pain. Suffering in the body helps take suffering off of the mind. If the mind breaks down that's the end of it. But the body can take a lot. So that's the balance G_d gave us, body and mind, or body and spirit.

Every Knock Is a Boost

The body takes a lot of burden off of the mind by bearing a lot of pain, or taking on a lot of pain. You can go farther worrying about your body than you can go worrying about your nerves or your mind. G_d is the best Knower. He knows how to manage His creation and none can manage it but Him. That's why we have to turn to Him. So, we should focus on G_d rather than the pain. G_d knows if He gives you enough pain, even though you have forgotten about Him for fifty years you are going to remember Him.

We're human and there's a spirit that's with us all of the time, but we just have to wake up to it. Sometimes, it's tragedy or physical pain that wakes us up to it. Those that are really with G_d and want to remain with Him, when they have those experiences, they benefit from those experiences. It makes them more conscious in the future. For the person that already has faith you see the lesson in the experiences. You get the lesson from the experiences and it helps you fare better with your life after that. For example, I've heard people from the South say, "Every knock is a boost!"

Loss of the Original Life

Science, the secular world, gives us history and theory on how man (the human being) formed on the earth and progressed. However, religion is not giving us a picture of flesh development. It is giving us a picture of community development, how the establishment of community life was designed into our very creation by G_d; that it is the natural heritage of every one of us to have and support community life.

The bird comes here and knows when it is time to have baby birds. It knows to start getting the straw and whatever to make a home for its babies. It knows how to make its home. No man taught the bird to make the home round and make it of this particular straw or soft, dry stuff. The bird knows that by virtue of its own creation. Its own life knows it. Its life as it came into existence knows that. So it will know what to do when time comes and it does it.

It is the same for humans. You don't have to teach a baby to crawl. It is going to crawl. We give them help but you don't have to teach the human baby to walk. It is going to walk because it sees you walking. You are not an English teacher but the baby learns to speak your language just by listening to you. So these are great developments. It is nothing to push aside. This is the beginning of life. It is clocked into our very composition as flesh people and it expresses itself, automatically, inside, when the time comes. When the situation presents itself there is the right response to the situation and it does what G_d has designed for it to do.

You know if we just depended on nothing but that original life, if people depended on nothing but that original life, we would be better off than we are right now, because at least we would learn to walk. We would come here ready to crawl, to walk and we would come here ready to learn how to love one another and be family. G_d clocked all of that into our creation, into our nature. Into our very flesh He put that. But the world deceives us and then we lose the original life. We lose the interest to be nice and loving to each other and the spirit to be family, not causing problems and suffering for each other; but working together in unity. In your education, your schooling, the academic world tells you that family is the first unit of society and that is what we have lost, family. This problem is not germane to any one group. It has taken over all people and all religions. All religious people are suffering the corruption of the family.

Obey G_d Even When in Difficulty

G_d says in the Qur'an, *"It is not that He wants to burden you, but He wants that you be purified .*[1] So that is what G_d tells us to position us to enjoy obeying Him even when it is difficult and we are suffering immensely. The real true believers, when we're doing something for G_d and we know He wants us to do it, it could be so heavy on the muscles or painful for the body or whatever, but we are not thinking about pain. G_d just takes the pain away from us and makes us unconscious of the difficulty and pain. He takes it away from us and all we are doing is enjoying doing what He wants us to do. Our reflection upon this helps us to understand better G_d's purpose for allowing us to have suffering, pain, and difficulty in our lives and it helps us to understand that the love and mercy of G_d is there for us at all times.

1

Bitterness of Life Necessary

We are given the story of Hajar (Hagar) searching, running back and forth between two hills, running over land and going through one elevation of the land on the one extreme and returning to another elevation of land on the opposite extreme. This is a picture of the ritual washing before prayer for Muslims, called wudu'. You wipe the hair in back of the head and then you come to the front. During the Pilgrimage (Hajj) we imitate Hajar running between the two hills searching for water for her child. One hill represents the front of the head and the other hill represents the back of the head. Safa is the front of the head and it's called suffering when you can't get results; and the back of the head is the Marwa. It sends you back to the front when it doesn't have enough to supply you with.

Hajar was running between those two hills, running over land. It was land all of the way and she is running over land. So running back and forth eventually brings a spark, like the little scouts do when they're rubbing sticks on a hard, dry surface. Going back and forth eventually created a spark. The friction created a spark and the spark was the Zamzam (the wellspring, or fountain that came up at the heel of Isma'il (Ishmael). The light was the Zamzam and it sprang up at the heels of Isma'il, peace be upon the Prophet.

There's another traditional part to this story that helps us to understand what happened. It says Hajar was desperately in need of water for her child and a little bird flew down, landed at the heels of Isma'il, and pecked the earth. When it pecked the earth a fountain sprang forth. This is in Islamic tradition. Now, all we know is what G_d says in the Qur'an, that she was running back and forth between the two hills; and we know that tradition tells us G_d answered her pleading, or desperate situation, by causing the Zamzam fountain to spring up.

Pictures and Stories to Teach

In fact, the same message is given over and over in Scripture, but in different ways, to give us more understanding of it in its more evolved or more progressed form. You see, this is the same situation that man was in when his world was very small in terms of development or knowledge. He even finds himself in that same situation when his world is more developed and evolved. But we need another description, or another language, to describe his situation in latter times as opposed to the earlier or former times. Nevertheless, it's still addressing, primarily, the same situation. That's why Scripture says that the little lamb came up and took a little book. He was able to digest the big book and condense it into a small book. He read it and the creatures marveled at the little lamb taking the book and breaking the seals. When you can see that this knowledge is being repeated that's how the seals are broken. It is repetitious and it's really evolving itself along with the evolving world.

Don't we use pictures and stories to teach young children? The Creator has created His man to make His man first see the reality of the world in which he lives in preschool language. But that preschool language, once he tries to understand it, decipher it, try to get what it's saying to him, is really university language. G_d is teaching with His creation.

Let's put ourselves back into the position of pre-science man, pre-modern science man. We're going back in time. We're going to stand in the position of prehistory man. Now, we're like the Prophet, Abraham, observing the universe to try to find out what the truth is. So, we see the sun coming up and we think, like all other people of that prehistory time that the sun actually sleeps in the earth at night and comes up in the day to light our world and serve our world. If you read the Bible in the New Testament, maybe even the Old Testament, you will know that men who were talking about the creation and about G_d were actually seeing the creation from this pre-science viewpoint, because they saw the sun as a symbol for their G_d. "Oh G_d! Why don't You show Your face? Oh G_d! Why do you sleep?" They're reading what they saw in the sun; that this world is under darkness. "Rise up, like the sun from your rest and light our world!"

World of Suffering Souls

We're talking about potential, the potential in the earth, in the heart of the earth. The heart of the earth means the potential in man's intellect. That's the point we're trying to establish. In Egyptian mythology, religious myth on the science of the dead, the living and hell, they believed that the sun came up out of the earth. They said, "The sun comes up and we see it and then it goes down and passes through the darkness under the earth and going through that darkness is the underworld." That's the underworld. It's the world of darkness and it's also the world of the suffering souls, the souls in torment and it has to free itself from that. So what keeps it going is trials, difficulty, while suffering all of that. It has to go through all of that to prepare it to rise, again.

Death Stimulates Life

Isn't this a belief of man? Many philosophers addressing the ups and downs of man's life say that the bitterness in his life is necessary to prepare him to appreciate the sweetness, to move him on to have an appetite strong for the sweetness. So suffering makes him stronger in his appetite for the sweetness and the sweetness pretty soon wears off, like the setting of the sun and puts him in trouble, again. He has to go through hell, again and the bitterness, again. One serves the other and the two regulate the whole so that man's life is continuous. Death, in that sense, stimulates life, or urges man to go to life, again, after he suffers his death so long. Then, the life gets born to him and he wants to rest. He rests too long and he finds himself in hell, again. This is like a rotation, i.e., the explanation for the life of the world, what keeps it going.

The Light of His Creation

"The sun, when it rises up, what should I read out of this? What message should I get out of this?" That's the thinker. He says, "What message should I get out of this?" He finally comes to the idea that the sun represents the light of his creation, the moral and rational light of his own creation; that it has to rise up out of his body. He comes to see himself as a microcosm[2] and the outer world as the macrocosm[3] and "Just as the sun has to break free of the chambers of the macrocosm, I have to break free of my ignorance". So it's about the conscious, the awakened mind, the mind waking up from its sleep in death or in the static world, the dead world; waking up from sleep. It comes up and it shines. In fact, it's a gradual light. It comes gradually. It's soft on the eyes at first. But when you see it, it's hard on the eyes, very bright and when it's very bright it's on your level. When it's hurting for you to look at it, it's on your level. You don't have a tendency to look at it when it's above your head. But when it's on your level, that's when you have a tendency to look at it. If you do, it's punishing to the eyes. So this is a sign of what? It is a sign of the educator, the person who is blessed with knowledge. When he first gets it he's not wise. So he tries to show himself to you on your level and if he tries to talk to you on your level it is too hard on your eyes.

Higher Levels of Human Form

Many of us don't have the consciousness of G_d we should have. If you have strong awareness of G_d then G_d is first in your life all the time. G_d is the most important thing in our life all of the time if we have G_d consciousness and our love for G_d is greater than our love for anybody else or anything else. It should be much greater than it is for anybody or anything else.

Consequently, when we give charity to assist those who are in difficulty, we shouldn't give it to impress somebody, or to be a savior for somebody. We should give charity because G_d says give charity and we should resist that feeling in ourselves to say, "I'm helping this person". We should resist that even though it's natural to be like that. G_d is raising us to higher and higher levels, so it's natural for you to be in that form on that level that was your natural human form. But G_d is going to raise you to higher levels of human form. There are higher levels of human form. He wants to raise you from that level to a higher level of human form where your ego is not always in play and you're not doing charity with awareness that you're helping somebody. You're doing charity with an awareness that G_d has made it possible for you to give this charity and, "I love G_d and He says give it".

You see, if we become like this, if we become strong in our awareness of G_d, we won't have to worry about attracting people. People will see us and they will love us. They will identify us as the righteous. They will love us and they will just come in great numbers. So, we must first have people that have the correct form that G_d wants.

2

Protecting the Innocent

In defining righteousness in the Qur'an G_d says in Chapter 2, *"It is not righteousness that you turn your faces East or West. But it is righteousness to believe in G_d and the Last Day and the angels and the book and the messengers; to spend out of your substance out of love for Him"*, out of love for G_d.[4] You see how close we are to Christians and other people of faith? The love of G_d is above all love; for your kin or on your kin, for orphans, for the needy, for the wayfarer, meaning the homeless, the person out of doors. They are people of the road, *"Wab nas sabeeli"*, meaning people of the road. But the term that's used is not, sharia, a common name for road. That tells us that it is not only for the person who is physically out of doors, who is physically without a home or a place to stay. But it is also for the person who is mentally out of doors and mentally without a home in which he can live and have peace, protection, security, privacy and production. So it is the mentally out of doors, the mentally homeless. When they brought African Americans from Africa, made us slaves here and cut us off from our past, they made all of us people mentally homeless, mentally out of doors. Mr. W. D. Fard (the teacher of the Honorable Elijah Mohammed) called us, "the mentally dead".

G_d goes on to say in Qur'an, *"For those who ask and for those who do not ask"*, like the ones we meet all the time in the community and out in the street. "Can you spare car fare or can you give me money for the bus? Can you help me with some food?" You say, "Well, he wants a drink". We should not come to that conclusion. Even though you feel positively sure in your heart, in your mind, that this person wants to get a drink, do not come to that conclusion. If you really think he is going to do that, give him some help if you can afford it and then tell him, "Be good to yourself. Don't hurt yourself". Do not deny him the help. Help him. Help him with the money and also help him with advice. Give him good advice. Pull him back from the wrong. But when you turn him down, give him no money and walk away cold you didn't even register his problems. You make him a worst drunk. You are contributing to his problem rather than helping him solve it. Maybe that's why he is out there, because people are cold and insensitive.

G_d Always in Charge

Continuing, G_d says, *"And for the ransom of slaves"*, to free slaves, to pay the price for their freedom, or spend for their freedom from slavery. *"And to be steadfast in prayer and practice regular charity.* The word here for charity is, zakat, and it is translated, regular charity. But zakat is a Qur'anic term. It was not always a term that the Arabs knew. They did not know the word, zakat. This was a new word. So we say it is an Arabic Qur'an. Yes, it is an Arabic Qur'an, but the Arabs themselves did not know many of the words in the Qur'an until they were revealed to Muhammed, peace be upon him. They did not have these words. Many of these words were not in their language until it was revealed to Muhammed. That is why the average Arab on the streets, now, who has not studied Islam, he reads the Qur'an and he does not know anything. The Qur'an is very difficult for him to read.

"And to fulfill contracts which you have made". This is righteousness. So if you make an agreement with somebody, you have to carry that out. You cannot back off from it and start giving all kinds of excuses, looking for loopholes, or some way out to keep you from answering your part of the deal, or the bargain. You cannot do that and be good believers.

"And to be firm and patient in pain, or suffering and adversity". So a sign of a righteous person, a believer and a righteous person when trouble comes is that the trouble doesn't take them over. Trouble comes but the trouble doesn't take them over. When you see people panicking, their faith was not there and certainly their righteousness was not there. No, we are never supposed to be disturbed like that. If we have strong consciousness of G_d we'll have faith in G_d. We will know that

no matter how bad the situation looks G_d is always in charge, always. We are only to do the best that we can because G_d has not made us angels or super creatures. So, what we cannot handle, if we feel satisfied that we have done our best, we are at peace. Our peace is not disturbed. Even if our mother is tormented on her death bed and squirming and paining that shouldn't make us squirm in pain. It shouldn't, no matter how good she was to us. No matter much we love her it shouldn't make us squirm in pain. It might draw a tear, but tears fall from a peaceful soul, not only from a disturbed soul. G_d, concludes this verse on righteousness by saying, *"Such are the people of truth, the G_d-fearing"*.

Righteousness and Fear of G_d

Many of us can be innocently going along in religion but truth has not yet been discovered as a very powerful part of our life and a very, very high value in the scale of our values. Some of us haven't discovered that. All this is about righteousness and it says, *"And they are the G_d fearing"*, having taqwa, strong taqwa. We conclude then that righteousness and taqwa (fearing and respecting G_d) go together. You cannot have righteousness without taqwa and you cannot have taqwa without righteousness.

So the righteous are not people who practice some kind of spiritual discipline to get close to G_d, to get close to the superior nature, or the superior reality and maybe become saintly in their life devoted only to spiritual matters and not caring about sex, etc. That's not righteousness. Righteousness is doing just what this verse says righteousness is, i.e., caring for people in our society, wanting to take misery out of the society; wanting to bring help to the people who want help; wanting to assist those who are weak and can't manage for themselves. This is righteousness and that's the righteousness of the Prophets in the Bible and in Scripture.

The Garden as an Inheritance

G_d says He made the Garden as an inheritance, the Garden of Paradise. Is this Garden somewhere near Iraq or somewhere else? Is this Garden a physical place? What is this Garden? G_d revealed to Muhammed and to us through him that the width of the Garden that He has for His servants is as the width of the heavens and the earth. So is this a garden that we plow with a sharp, heavy piece of wood like they did in primitive times for industry? No, we plow this garden with our intellectual curiosities. We search G_d's creation and He says He made the whole world to yield its benefits to the human family, the human community, or to Adam, meaning all the human family. He made this creation to yield its benefits. If you know what He's speaking of, G_d is speaking of whatever is in the sky and the earth.

Astronomers, they study what is in the sky, the stars, their pattern of movement, etc. and many other things. They studied about the heavenly bodies and they grew the science of astronomy. The farmer studied the land and how it benefits and supports different kinds of crops and he became a scientist of agriculture and we progress that way. So this Garden, G_d says He made it as an inheritance. That means you don't have to have it and you don't have to have the sense to get it. G_d created you and you're going to interact with people, human beings, who have needs. You're going to seek to answer those needs and find the answers in the earth and in His matter that He created in the creation. You are going to find the answers there. You're going to plow His creation with your intellect and you're going to bring much production and much development to the human family. So this is how we should see these things in order for us to make progress in these days and times.

Guardians Over Us

We used to have guardians over us. They were decent human beings, people who made themselves guardians to protect the ignorant people and to press for better conditions for the masses of suffering people. We don't have guardians like that anymore. Satan has taken over the management of our appetite for pleasure. We have very few and their efforts are so small. So we pray that G_d in His mercy blesses us with guardians, again, who will work in our world to protect the innocent and to remove the burden of ignorance from our suffering masses.

3

———————

Nothing Between Mistreated and G_d

I tend to be a little philosophical and many things clear up for me when I try to see it philosophically. I think nations or continents of people come into life just like a human individual comes into life. If they have a lot of freedom, a lot of authority to express themselves and live like they want to live, they reach a point where they don't want that anymore. That goes into their spirit and consequently many will stop competing and give up the struggle. They stop competing. They get out of the race. They're satisfied. "Oh, I've lived enough. I've seen my day. I've had my best days".

I think that is what happens to nations and I believe that's what happened to Africa. Africa is an old nation and an old continent; maybe the oldest. We don't know. I think when people have lived their glorious days a long time it's not in their spirit anymore to compete with other civilizations. That was not good for Africa.

I think that G_d brought us (African Americans) here to this country. We came by a terrible route, pain and suffering and everything, but I think G_d brought us here. I believe the purpose for being brought here was that we be denied the life and consequently, we would have a thirst for life, again; and a thirst for being builders, again; a strong desire to be builders, again. Now the new children of Africa in America will have this and I think we're going to spark them (Africans) from here, from this side. I don't want to see our people turn to Africa because really I've been there and they need our help. It's not much they can offer us. But, we can offer them a lot.

The whole orderly picture of the material world, its objects in the sky, in the earth, all exist as a womb. Taken all together or separately it exists as a womb, or support communicating to man his life and life functions. As Native Americans have it and I'm quoting their wise men's words, "Every part of it (meaning the objective world) holds a message for the human being and human society."

These are the Native Americans that we write off. Don't think they are not wise. "Oh, they are savage and the white man conquered them". No, not yet. They are still defying them. That tells me that they are not completely conquered, yet. They are still defiant and their wise men have told them, "Don't give in to Western civilization. We will outlive them and you will have your life back, again."

So they tell their children that when they're born. They want to see who is going to be a chief, or who is going to be wise. When they find one mind they can trust they pass it on to that child. "You have been selected". It stays among them generation after generation and they are not going to give it up. They will be with it until G_d changes this world.

Preserving Logic for Your Life

They are wise. They are faithful. They are human. They are little giants, their wise ones. Do not underestimate these people that the white man (the West) conquered. Hasn't the West also conquered the following of Muhammed? They certainly have. Are we uncivilized? Are we stupid? No! Do we have a survival plan like the Native American? I don't see it. We keep deteriorating. The Islamic world keeps deteriorating. Where is our survival plan? At least we don't see the native Indian deteriorating. He's holding on and he's now where he was when the white man came. In fact, he's wiser. Speaking for them as a whole or the majority of them, they are wiser than they were before the white man came. But they still have the same determination to preserve their own identity and to preserve your identity you must preserve the logic for your life and not give it up for anything. That is how you preserve your identity.

Believe me it hurt my heart seeing how they were treated and how they suffered. It hurt my heart seeing them held back from the benefits of civilization, of industrial world comforts, education and everything. It still hurts my heart. But when I really saw their plan and their determination, that pain went away. I don't have that pain in my heart for them anymore. They are little giants and they are not as bad off as the world thinks they are. They have a survival plan and are not giving it up. I wish they could see Al-Islam. Al-Islam is their property. Al-Islam is their inheritance just as it is ours.

Nothing Between Mistreated and Lord

It is reported that Prophet Muhammed said there is nothing between the mistreated one and his Lord, not even something as thin as a veil; no partition between the mistreated human person and his G_d. G_d does not put anything in the way of the suffering person and his Lord.

G_d created the human being and He doesn't need the learned world to save the human being. They are not going be successful in trying to lock human beings out of the life G_d created them for. Jesus ended up being the victor. The Bible says they crucified him but their own lands have been taken over by Jesus' followers of that land. Even the Jews had to be helped by followers of Jesus Christ. Muhammed, nobody helped him. But out of the Arabs came a teacher, a leader, helped by no one.

Here we were in America denied entrance to places that could help us qualify to compete and now the bottom rail is rising to the top. Colin Powell, his people were put on the bottom and are now going to the top. The slaves themselves, their lot like Elijah Mohammed, i.e., uneducated, poor language and from them comes Imam W. Deen Mohammed who loves science and loves to go abroad. My father said, "You're the one I wanted to go abroad".

Good News Bringer

Bashirun means, mortal being and bashir refers to the human being as a sensitive human being with flesh covered with skin. It refers to the skin of the human being and then G_d gives the Prophet a title, Bashir, after the same word. But do not say, "Mortal". As a title bashir means, "Good news bringer".

What is the meaning of good news bringer? It is that a man is told now he has become a messenger because of his sensitive nature, or his sensitive skin. You won't become a messenger unless you feel for others. You have to register their difficulties, their needs, etc., and then G_d will make you a messenger. If a messenger is needed, He will pick a person like that to be His messenger. In his feelings he registers the feelings, the needs, the suffering of others and that is the last level or step in the creation of the mortal. In the Qur'an it says, "Bone, flesh and thereafter another creature". That is the sensitive creature with skin, human feelings. That is what G_d is saying.

That is the good news, that it is not something foreign to my nature that G_d gives me as a guide. It is my own nature that G_d gives me as a guide. That is good news for the scholars. They don't like something that seems illogical or something that does not recognize the human being. What evolved man's mind was his recognition that he is created different from all of these other things; that he is a special creation high above the other things that he sees in his environment. You bring something that puts that down and that is bad news. For thousands of years man has been marveling over his own creation that is much higher than other creation and then the news comes that you are a sinner. You're born with sin and a supernatural has to come and save you from your sin, because you are not good enough in your body to be saved by someone of your nature. That is bad news.

Empathy for Others

We should be more numerous, the believers, the good people. G_d has not made more people hard-hearted, callous. He has made most us more empathetic and has made fewer people apathetic, not caring about other people suffering, not feeling the hurt of others. G_d has made most of us to empathize, to have empathy, to see other human beings' suffering and feel it. He made us to put our self in the other person's place and share the burden with them.

Now, you are suffering, too. Although you didn't have it happen to you, personally, what happened to them, but now you're suffering as well. You see how G_d made us to pull us into their suffering? "Now, I'm uncomfortable, too. So I have an issue, too, with you. You have hurt this man and his hurt is on me". So when enough of us are hurt we're going to do something about it. We're going to come to the rescue of that person who was dealt injustice. This is how G_d has made us and more of us are like that than not. But why is it that we don't have the great majority, then, standing up for right, or standing up for justice?

The Voice of G_d

We are the minority in number because we have been misguided by the Satan and his followers. He misguides the good people and he robs them of their numbers. They're still human. They're still kind-natured. But he has overpowered them, influenced them to go astray, to go away from their nature, to be in opposition to their own nature. So they join him in spreading cruelty instead of kindness, making the world miserable instead of making it comfortable and pleasant. But they are not really his. He has stolen them from humanity. He has stolen them from G_d. That means it is possible that we can get them back. It is possible that we can get a majority and the great civilized nations they believe in majority. They believe that the majority's will is good and they are not believing something that others before didn't believe. In Al-Islam it says, "G_d's control is on the group". It is on the community, not on individuals. That means the collective body is ultimately the voice of G_d.

Civilized nations respect the will of the people, the will of the nation. If they determine that the position that their nation has taken expresses the will of the people they respect it. Although other interests may cause them to eventually violate what they respect, initially, they do respect it. They acknowledge that it is the will of the people. Those who want to keep a cruel control or cruel hand over the people or on the people will confuse those outside and make them think that the people's will is different from what it really is. However, in time the truth is made known and the will of the people has to be recognized.

Individual Will by G_d's Permission

G_d says in the Qur'an, *"You shall not will, except as G_d wills"*.[5] We cannot do anything. We cannot have it our way, except as G_d wills. G_d wills that we be human beings like we are. G_d wills that we have the life we have and the privileges we have, etc. G_d has willed that and it couldn't be any other way, because that is G_d's Will. What you think your will is will be carried out, maybe. But more importantly, it is also G_d's will carried out, because nothing can happen except as G_d wills. This is Scripture. This is the Qur'an and other Scriptures, too. Nothing can happen except as G_d wills.

4

"No Eye Has Seen, No Ear Has Heard"

People are only at fault if they have knowledge. So that's why in Al-Islam once you become a Muslim, the past is forgiven. Whatever you did in the past is forgiven. Your record starts from that point and of course G_d says in the Qur'an, "Never did We destroy a people before sending a warner to them." That's because they haven't had a chance! They are not completely responsible for the situation. Consequently, they don't have the biggest share in the responsibility for their situation. Those before them have a bigger share. So shouldn't they get help? Someone might say, "Oh, whatever happens to you in this life, that's it. Once you die, that's the end of it. You can't be punished beyond that". To believe like that is not to follow the word of G_d. To believe like that is to take it upon yourself to define reality. That's too much, that statement.

"No Eye Has Seen, No Ear Has Heard"

I don't know what the afterlife will be, but I've invested in it. I have faith! Believe me, if it's nothing I'm happy. If it's nothing, if this is the end of it, nothing else coming, I'm happy. It wouldn't change my position. I would still be working just the same. You and I wouldn't change at all, except maybe for the better because we've invested in that. That's where iman (faith) comes in. We have to have faith. So I've invested in that and I know that something is going to come. But will it be something resembling what I can imagine? I don't know. Maybe it will be. But the Prophet Muhammed said, "Of that no eye has seen, no ear has heard". So this paradise with wives having big, wide eyes, rich foliage and fruit hanging within close reach, that's not descriptive of what we've got in mind. That's descriptive of what we're to get on this earth, G_d willing. That's how you have to understand it, because that's how the Prophet taught it.

Long Road of Suffering a Test

The Qur'an says, *"Would Thou destroy us for that which the ignorant among us did? It is but by trial"*.[6] Isn't this wonderful? Here is a human mortal who has suffered great abuse and misguidance for generations. He has died in this state and still he remains faithful to G_d. So when he sees the light he interprets the abuses and his suffering as trials and he says, "This was just to try me." He says, *"It is but a trial. Thou sendeth whom Thou will astray and guideth whom Thou will. Thou art our Protecting Friend. Therefore, forgive us and have mercy on us. Thou art the best of those to show mercy".*[7] This is very beautiful, especially when you understand it; that man is accepting his long road of suffering, misery, etc., as a test from G_d and by the test he is improved.

It is like what the ancients used to do. They would put the coarse metal in the fire and the fire refined it. If you've worked with metal, you know that sometimes you have to hit the metal with a hammer. You put it in a confinement. You put it in a mold, imprison it. You have to torture it with the heat. You choke it to make wire. You do everything with it. Then, you hammer it with a big, long hammer. You hit it, burn it and beat it so it doesn't crack, because metal tends to crack when it's cooling quickly. You beat it while it's still hot so that it won't crack. You see, all of these things have meaning. G_d has told us in the Qur'an that all of these things have meaning. So, man sees it as his trial, something that G_d has designed to make him better, to improve him.

It goes on to say, *"And ordain for us in this world that which is good and in the Hereafter that which is good. Lo, we have turned unto Thee."* And G_d says, *"I smite with My punishment whom I will and My mercy embraces all things"*.[8] Isn't that wonderful? He smites with His punishment whom He wills. That means that some people will be spared punishment. Don't think everybody is going to be punished; not in the way you're thinking they are going to be punished. It's left up to the mercy of G_d. You see how we relieve ourselves of a lot of burden that's not necessary? Don't run around here carrying the world on your shoulders. Some things you have to just see and keep on going.

We Judge Ourselves Too Much

So the guidance of G_d is our salvation. The guidance is a mercy because it enables us to see our limitations in creation and to accept what is beyond human capacities as the planning of G_d. The guidance of G_d enables you to do what G_d has qualified you to do, what G_d has given you the power to do; and do the measure of that and be happy. You know, you can have a good life if you live that way? I mean even in our own homes we want to see our children progress. We want a bright child. "I want an exceptional child". But if you don't accept G_d and that His Will may not be your will, you will go crazy.

So you see we judge ourselves too much. We should apply this kind of reasoning in all circles of life. Yes, do your best and when you have done your best, relax, be happy. I always tell people that, "Look, I can't talk to you while you're emotional like that". I told a boy, "I can't talk to you while you're emotional like that. You're going to have to settle down. It isn't that bad". I said, "What you're doing is looking only on the outside".

In the Bible, the Old Testament, the Prophet speaks of his fast and he says his fast is to serve the suffering, help those who are suffering to relieve their miseries. That was his fast. We know our fast is for G_d, but G_d says, "What you offer Me does not reach Me. Only your obedience reaches Me". G_d loves your obedience because He knows your obedience is going to make you a better creation and a much more useful creation to yourself and to others, especially to your family. G_d knows that.

G_d says only your obedience reaches Him. If only my obedience reaches my G_d then who is benefiting, directly? Nothing can benefit G_d. Benefit means you added something. G_d has everything. No matter what we give Him we are not giving Him anything because He already has everything. So who is benefiting? We are benefitting. The fasting person benefits and he is made a better, more conscious person, more sympathetic person, when suffering in others is noticed or observed.

Closer to What G_d Wants

So our fast is not different in terms of where the benefits go or who benefits. It is not different from the fast of the Prophets of the Old Testament or the fast of the faithful religious people in the Old and New Testaments; and even other books ought to be included other than the Bible and the Qur'an. Fasting benefits the individual, helping the individual to know the suffering of the poor. The fasting person says, "I guess this is how my neighbor feels all the time." You know he's hungry. He's poor and not eating good, so you become aware of the pain that he's experiences all the time, maybe every day. But this fasting (abstaining from food and drink during daylight hours) is something you volunteer to do for G_d's sake for one month out of the year; and it increases your awareness of the difficulties of others who are not voluntarily abstaining from food and drink. They can't help it.

In the month of fasting (Ramadan) great charity goes to the suffering people. If you cannot fast the month, if you have the means, then you feed sixty persons. We know that at the end of the fast month we go to the Eid Prayer and before we join the congregation for the Eid Prayer we give money for those who are not fortunate enough to have it or to have the means. We give what is called sadaqa, the gift or charity for the Eid. Eid means the celebration day.

So our fasting is for G_d so that we have the spirit or our obedience comes closer and closer to what G_d wants of us. And it is expected that we will help others who are suffering, share with them our food, our drink, our earnings, so that misery and suffering becomes less and less in the community of mankind.

Matters Judged by Intentions

Muslims are all over the world. Al-Islam began in Mecca, Arabia, the land of the Arabs, in the dust, in the sand. Since then it has gone, firstly, to Africa, to the Mediterranean area and finally to Spain and Europe; and preachers have now taken the religion of Al-Islam all around the world. In Europe, Canada, South America, the United States and everywhere there are Muslims and there are Christians, too. All over the world, we find big followings of the religions that are called, the heavenly religions.

Why are they called the heavenly religions? It is because we believe that G_d sent His word down to human beings and He chose righteous servants of excellent character and nature to deposit His words into them so that they would give His word to others, to believers in revelation. We believe that G_d reveals, G_d communicates, G_d talks to human beings. So we are called heavenly faiths or heavenly religions; Judaism, Christianity, Al-Islam and perhaps some others. These are the major ones, the most noticeable ones.

The nature of obedience for Christians, Muslims, Jews and many others that we don't know about is, perhaps, the same. The nature is to give ourselves to G_d and if our intent is good we are accepted by G_d. You may not know G_d as Muslims know G_d. But if your intent is good you are accepted by G_d. If your intent is bad you are going to hell and G_d doesn't care for you at all. Muhammed, the Prophet, said, "Matters are judged by intentions." I know many of us are good-hearted people. But we have some bad-hearted habits, thinking we are the only ones righteous because we are Muslim; or, we are the only ones who have the religion right because we are Muslims. That doesn't necessarily have to be so. In order for us to have the right picture of Al-Islam we have to have good intentions and the right heart.

If your heart is right you don't enjoy seeing other people suffer no matter what their religion is.

If Soul Spoiled Everything Else Is

If your heart is right you don't feel happy only when you make a big buck. You are happy when your brother, your sister, or even just another human being makes a big buck. We have to learn to rejoice, to feel good upon seeing others lifted up or made richer.

We have been poor for a long time. We have been poor for longer than we have been living. We have inherited and acquired it. It is deep down inside of me because I lived in my father and he was poor. I lived in his father and he was poor. If you could go back and back in time, you would be aware that you have been poor for many lifetimes. So, you aren't happy to see other people getting over and you aren't. Sometimes it is your brother in your own family and you say, "Why did it have to be him?" We have to get rid of that. It is not you. That is your mistake. It is not really you.

If we had the chance to think it over we would really feel good about what others are enjoying. We would share in their enjoyment. But it is a bad habit that we have when we say, "I wonder how he got that new car? I'll bet he paid fifty thousand dollars for a car like that." That shouldn't even interest you. The only car you should be interested in how much it costs is the car you buy, because you have to have enough money to pay for it.

The Arabs have been influenced by Al-Islam to come up with the expression, "Don't try to look into the cooking pot of your neighbor." The neighbor's cooking pot is the neighbor's business. That does not only mean do not look into the cooking pot. But it also means don't look and peep trying to see what somebody else has because it spoils the soul. And if the soul is spoiled everything else eventually is spoiled; that is, the way you think, the way you behave.

5

True Religion Goes After the Mistreated

G_d says in the Qur'an of Muhammed, the Prophet, when he was noticed by other people carrying out his responsibility to his Lord, his G_d, *"We have heard a caller calling to faith and we have responded saying, 'We believe. We have faith'".*[9] Why does G_d have it like that for us? It is to let us know that the invitation to Al-Islam is first the invitation to faith. Many who have become Muslims when they are giving the greeting, it sounds like they are Muslims and they are, I believe, in their innocence. But they do not have faith. If they had faith we who have faith would know it. A believer in G_d knows another believer in G_d. You can't disguise yourself.

G_d Is Real

A believer in G_d readily knows another believer in G_d. So don't think they're not seen. We know every one that we meet who does not have faith. In fact, you don't have to meet them. We can be sitting in the same room with them, hear their conversation and know they don't have faith. That is the first step in Al-Islam, faith. You should be, firstly, a believer in the G_d Who made everything. For Muslims and for others, too, the point is clear and strong that we are not to believe in superstitions. We don't have faith supported or based upon superstition, some spooky idea of the existence of G_d. G_d is no spook. G_d is real.

G_d is, first of all, goodness. G_d is truth and G_d is intelligence. G_d is not playing games. G_d is not playing games with you or with me, watching us to see if we take some water in our mouth or a piece of candy when we're supposed to be fasting. No, G_d is too big for that petty thing. He created you to watch over yourself and when you don't watch yourself He is not worried about you.

Our faith is an intelligent faith. That is the point. It is not a hocus pocus faith. It is not a faith based upon some spooky idea or spooky thing. We're not spooked up. We're not scared into wanting to be obedient to G_d. We were attracted by G_d's beauty, by G_d's goodness, by G_d's love, by G_d's generosity. We were attracted to want to believe in G_d and obey G_d because we think we owe that to Him. He has given us so much and we owe it to Him to give Him obedience. The sun, moon and stars give their obedience to the Lord Who gave them their logic, Who set them on a course that is logic and logical. Their order in the sky is scientific. Their nature is scientific. It is intelligent. It is governed by laws. These laws are consistent, intelligent and reflect or communicate to the thinking, obedient soul, G_d's will, G_d's purpose, what G_d wants. This is Islamic thought that I'm sharing with you. If G_d made the universe to obey Him, how stupid it would be for us to disagree with the order of the universe.

True Religion Goes After the Suffering

In the Bible Jesus Christ said he'd knock the dust off of his feet. If they rejected him he would leave the town. It says, *"But pity on them if he knocks the dust off his feet"*.[10] It means he was lifting up the people who didn't have any material establishment. They were like dust and could be blown or taken away by the breath, or by the spirit. So if they were not going to let him carry the dust, or the poor and ignorant people, he said he would knock it off, leave them there with them; and it would be worse than Sodom and Gomorrah what would come behind him.

That's what religion does. True religion goes after the suffering people and tries to take them off of the ground and put them in a better position to make something out of their lives, do something with their lives. If you prevent that kind of a messianic leader or that kind of preacher from doing his work, then that nation that leaves them without someone to gather them and do something with their lives will be threatened by those people, that element in their society. Eventually, it will cause their downfall.

The feet represent the spiritual people and it's the spirit that holds up everything. The poor people, they are in the feet. The spiritual teacher gathers the poor people. They respond. He gathers them and they are like dust on his feet. But his foundation is not dust. His foundation is spirit.

A Word and Spirit from G_d

Jesus Christ was the Spirit of G_d and a Word from G_d. So his spirit was very strong and also with the spirit is faith. Faith, spirit, and the Word of G_d which guides him, that's in the foundation. But now, if he goes away from that foundation and the dust goes away and is left back there with the people he's leaving, then they're in serious trouble. That's what the Bible is saying, that his coming and taking up the cause of the poor, suffering, ignorant people is what spares great nations and great powers; and it does. But they have always had a way of managing the spiritual crowd, or those people who have spirit but no knowledge and guidance. The ancients have always had a way to contain them and hold them. Baal is one of them. G_d calls it, "Baal", in the Bible, B-a-a-l.

So one way is pictured in the story of Baal riding the donkey until the donkey saw an angel with a flaming sword; a messenger with a flaming sword; or with the Word of G_d that's like a flaming sword; a sword that lights up. It doesn't only cut, but it lights. It's a light, also. It cuts and slays, but it's a light, also. That's the Word of G_d. So the donkey saw this angel holding the flaming sword in the pathway, in the way that it was traveling with its master on its back. The donkey said, "Why have you struck me these three times?" It says he spoke with a man's voice, so he is not a donkey anymore. The donkey spoke with a man's voice and he said, "Why have you struck me these three times"? [11]

"Only One"

That is answered in Bilal in the time of Muhammed, the Prophet. Bilal was a slave to his master and he was refusing to obey his master. That's asking his master, "Why have you struck me these three times? Why have you put my whole future in slavery, my flesh, my mind, and my spirit?" His way was just to protest slavery and for doing that his master put him in the hot sun. Jesus was put in the heat, too. So they put him (Bilal) in the hot sun and then put a heavy stone on his back. They thought that that would make him break and decide to give up his interest in Prophet Muhammed's call to Islam. But when he couldn't speak, he just held out one finger. He was so miserable he couldn't even speak. He just put up one finger, telling the one who insisted he believe in more than one G_d that he still believed in one G_d. He said, "Ahad, only One!" Finally, one from the Muslim side, a friend of Prophet Muhammed, Abu Bakr, came and paid his ransom, which shows that the master's interest was in money. The reason he had a person as a slave was because the slave was making money for him. So when the money came in an amount big enough he gave up that slave. After all, he had lost him anyway. [12]

Education Is the Answer

Bilal then is actually the answer to the Scripture that portrays the poor and ignorant people as a donkey and that one day the donkey would speak with a man's voice. So the call to Islam doesn't accept that people be ruled through their spirit, or by psychology; but that they be free to be educated; that education is the answer.

It started way back in the time of Noah. Noah had three sons. Ham was Egypt and was the one that showed ignorance. He wasn't uneducated, but his character was that of nafsil la ammara, the compulsive self, or the impulsive self. The impulsive self couldn't handle human conditions intelligently, laughing at the condition of the person rather than responding to the need in that person. The other two brothers responded to the need in the person, their father, Noah. But Ham did not. The Bible says he laughed and the curse fell on the children of Ham. That only means that if that disposition, silly disposition, gets into people it's going to be passed on to their children; and that is what happened. The poor, ignorant people, when they have children, their children come up behaving just like them, until one rebels, or sees a way out of it, or sees that it is wrong. His character is too strong to take it and he leaves it. He departs from his parents or his society.　But in most cases it's passed down from parents to children like that.

6

The Good News

Whenever you read the Qur'an, before you begin reciting you are to say, "I seek refuge with G_d from the enemy, Shaytan (Satan)." Every chapter except the 9th chapter of Qur'an, "Tauba (Repentance)", opens up, "With G_d's Name, the Merciful Benefactor, the Merciful Redeemer". What is the main subject of the 9th chapter? What is the main activity? What is going on more than anything else in the 9th chapter? It is war. People who take up war they are not in a condition to perceive G_d and His beauty. That is why the Old Testament shows you G_d in His anger most of the time.

It is all about conflict. The righteous are trying to survive the wicked. You are not inclined to think of G_d as, "The Merciful Benefactor, the Merciful Redeemer", or to think to say, "With G_d's Name, the Merciful Benefactor, the Merciful Redeemer", when you're fighting. You are not inclined to do that.

The religion of Islam shows the human nature in its picture that is accepted by G_d. If your life is threatened and you are fighting, G_d does not expect for you to say, "With G_d's Name, the Merciful Benefactor, the Merciful Redeemer." You are trying to save your life from an enemy who is trying to kill you or your family. He's trying to destroy your city, your town. What is G_d saying when He is revealing this chapter to us without the saying, "With G_d's Name, the Merciful Benefactor, the Merciful Redeemer?" He is saying that when mankind is at war with each other they are not saying, "With G_d's Name, the Merciful Benefactor, the Merciful Redeemer", and they are not expected to say that. They are fighting for their own survival, to save their own life. So G_d doesn't expect that. G_d forgives them for forgetting Him in such circumstances. But after they fight, get into trouble, lose lives and they begin suffering a lot, then they remember G_d. When things get hot and tough then they remember G_d.

So inside of Chapter 9 is a verse that says, *"With G_d's Name the Merciful Benefactor, the Merciful Redeemer"*, though it is not in the beginning; meaning when man gets into enough trouble, even though he is fighting and killing to save his own life, he will turn to his G_d. Isn't that nice, that you do not open the chapter or the subject of war with the name of G_d? G_d is saying, "I'm not with your war. You do not start your war with Me. You start your war on your own. But eventually you will turn to Me. When you catch enough hell, then you will remember Me; that I am the Merciful Benefactor, the Merciful Redeemer".

End of Suffering and Confusion

We want to make progress in the world. We don't want to fail. The first step then is to begin in your innocence. We want to get to the end of the road. The end of the road is not the end of living. The end of the road is the end of struggle, suffering and confusion. The end of the road is a good life here on earth and hereafter; a good life where you will feel good about yourself. You will be able to feel good about how you and your family are living. You will be able to feel good about how your neighborhood is striving or existing. Now how can you feel perfectly good as long as there is another neighborhood suffering like ours used to suffer, or there is another nation suffering like ours used to suffer? So you see G_d has created us to be one family, to register the hurt of all people, to feel their hurt and to not be comfortable in our souls until everybody has a life that is livable.

We know all of us are not this conscious. We practice putting things out of our mind that bother our conscience. We practice it so much until we can look at people suffering and crying, moaning, dying and being mistreated and we'll just keep on smiling, go to sleep and rest good tonight. But there are a few that G_d has created who won't accept that and one day from the few will come one who will disturb your rest, calling you out into the field to go to work to make things better. This is the way of G_d.

Progress on Road of Life

The second step, if you want a good life, is to make up in your mind to think, "Yes, I want a good life. I don't want a life that I have to be ashamed of. I want to be of good character. I don't want to be of bad character. I want to be somebody that other good people can feel comfortable around or with. I want to be a person that good people can trust. I want to be loved by my family and appreciated by my family". If you are that kind of person you have already made the first step. That tells us that your life is in good condition. The life G_d gave you is in good condition. Your temple is in good order, the temple of your flesh body.

So you want to be informed in order for you to make progress on the road of life. As I said, it is not for just anybody. You can't make progress on this road without being educated. You have to be educated and I'm not speaking of the academic world. I'm talking about good common sense and knowledge of how G_d made life or made you to live. That is what you have to have. We call it, G_d. You may not call it G_d. If you don't want to call it G_d, call it Creation. Call it Mother Nature. Call it whatever you want, but Something is responsible for making you the way you are and making you the human being you are. It created matter, nature, to give birth to you the first time. So if you don't want to include G_d, start right there with Mother Nature and say, "I want to be the best that Mother Nature offers me". Then say, "I want to see what direction, what help is in Mother Nature for my mind, for my reasoning, so I can reason better; so that my reasoning will serve me better and I can become more successful". Mother Nature is a teacher herself, isn't she? She is our first teacher.

Good News

Muhammed, the Prophet, was not stupid. When G_d called him he was a successful business man. He was not immoral or indecent. When he was called he was already a decent, moral and admired human being. His own people called him, as-Saadiq, the Truthful One and they called him, al-Amin, the Trustworthy One, the Honest One, the one that you can trust. They were calling him these names before G_d called him to be the Messenger of G_d.[13] What does that tell us? G_d is telling us by revealing to Muhammed the same thing that Jesus Christ in his sign, in his mystery tells us; that a human being can have a good life without revelation, without a Prophet being sent to them. G_d doesn't have to come to us that way. G_d made us to have a good life. If we would just respect the good life that G_d made for us we could have a good life as Muhammed had a good life; and he's just one example that is given to us. There were many human beings that became very decent, kept a good life and they became very rational, very intelligent and very productive without joining a religion. This is a fact of history and a fact of nature. Isn't that good news?

For the Christians this same message is in the nativity, the birth of Jesus Christ, but it is shrouded in mystery. The same message is coming to the Christian world that I am giving you right now and that is why the New Testament is called, "The Good News". These phonies in religion are telling people, "You have to repent, repent! You have to reject this mortal flesh, this mortal nature, reject this gross body! It is temptation that will lead you to damnation!" But the good news is that they got off track. They went blind in their own self-righteousness. The good news is human beings are born good and it is only your wrong thinking that makes you bad. That is the good news, that we all should have salvation. We have to learn to trust our good senses, our natural good intelligence that G_d created us with. We want to become more intelligent, more informed in the ways of life, in the ways of living successfully.

Serve Something Bigger

The third step is to struggle to know, "What is my purpose in this plan that I find in Mother Nature? I've found this big plan, now what is my purpose here? Am I to worship matter? Am I to worship the earth? Am I to worship the trees?" Then, you have to begin to search. You have to search the things you know to see if those things are worthy of you worshiping them, or you coming under them. But, if you search without revelation, without G_d, if you search with your good natural intelligence, you are going to come to the conclusion that, "I can't manage this by myself. I have to serve something above me". You can call it an idea or truth. You can call it a perception of your destiny. Call it whatever you want, but you have to serve something bigger than you.

G_d tells us in the Holy Qur'an, *"Oh man, don't think that the creation of a human being is a bigger matter than the creation of the skies and the earth."*[14] This world will overwhelm you. This world will beat you down, bury you and wipe your history out as though you never existed. That is what this world will do. It is a bigger matter than you. So at least find that discipline that accounts for this world being sustained. Find that discipline that sustains matter, the earth, Mother Nature's work or order and then say to yourself, "This world that is bigger than me is sustained by obedience to certain laws. So I am going to have to recognize a set of rules, a set of laws. There is something governing me that is bigger than my mind". Call it what you want, but that will be your salvation.

7

Rebirth of the World

G_d is Merciful, twice, to human life. First of all, He is Merciful by giving us mothers who will support us having a good life. We leave mother and go out thinking that we know it all and get into trouble and make the world miserable. Then, He chooses one who did not spoil things, that is, Muhammed, or someone like him and gives him revelation. That is the second mercy. This is the G_d Who is merciful, twice.

The second mercy, in my opinion, is a mercy that saves us. So, I call it redeeming, or redemptive mercy. I call G_d, the Redeemer and the mercy is redemptive mercy as in Christianity. That expression is also in Christianity. He is redeeming that which is lost. The first mercy that He gives we lose it. Then, He gives us a second chance. There is an expression in English, "Everyone deserves a second chance." Well, G_d gives us a second chance. The life was lost from that first mercy, so He redeems it and reconciles it with the first mercy. The good life that He created us for, He gives it to every baby that is born, unless the baby is born with a defect.

Living Against Our Nature

I have been studying for a long time defects in children, what they call natural defects or birth defects. When I started studying there was not nearly enough support for what I believed. But science now has a lot of support for what I believed many years ago. I believed that G_d made us all without defects and in time we messed up our life so much by living against our own good nature that we created birth defects. I don't believe we had birth defects to begin with. I believe G_d created the human being without birth defects, originally.

I believe we caused animals to have birth defects by poisoning the environment, messing with and confusing nature. G_d says in the Qur'an, *"Do not change the good nature created by G_d".*[15] You are not supposed to make alterations on it. But scientists are encouraged by industry and big business to experiment on nature no matter what the consequences are. They take chances on it and right now they are trying to come up with a way to alter even our genes, to even interfere with the way we are born.

Support against science being bold like that is in Scripture, the Bible and Qur'an and a lot of support has been discovered since I have been living. I have identified these mercies with nature and revelation. Our good nature is G_d's first mercy to us. He gave us good nature and we rebelled against it. And something inside tells us, if it's nothing but a bad feeling we are having, "That's wrong!" That's your good nature. That's that first mercy. That is what G_d gave you, i.e., the first mercy; the feeling inside that says, "I should not have done that", or "I should not be doing this." Sometimes it is fear. You feel afraid. You were going to do something and you feel afraid to do it. That is that good nature. However, we go on and do it, like the man called, Evil Knievel. I know he felt afraid before he started his daredevil business.

So Revelation is the second mercy and in the Bible G_d told the people who were believing in Him, *"I will give you a second portion of My Mercy"*.[16] Nature itself can take you only so far. Human nature and the natural world can only take you so far. Then, to open it up to go farther with science and civilization, G_d has to give us revelation.

Science Came Because of Revelation

There is no proof in the world that I know of that science came without Revelation, because even the earliest men that they call primitive and savage had some fear in them of a superior, or Supreme Being. When you do not have in you a desire to know causes behind effects you cannot carry civilization forward. The first cause that we want to know that's behind effect is: What caused this world to be? Man did not just have that with the Bible and the Qur'an. The earliest man on this planet had that because he was in fear of thunder, in fear of lightning and in fear of others.

Fear Makes You Believe

Fear makes you cry out to something. Fear makes you believe that there is a power bigger than you. You may call it the sun. You may call it lightning. You may call it any name. That is your ignorance until you grow better in your understanding. That is your ignorance that is saying G_d is the thunder or G_d is the lightning. At least the nature is in you to pray to something greater than yourself and it's in you when you are born.

The earliest people that they call savages had that in them and I read how science believes certain things were discovered, like metals. It says the lightning struck the ground, or the mountain side and burned the ore and the early people in development observed this phenomenon. They call them savages but I don't call them that. I call them early people in development. These people found that the lightning had created metals. It had burned the iron ore and made hard metals and they learned how to put fire to the ore and make metal. They learned how to take fire and put it to the metal that G_d gave them. G_d says, *"And He revealed the iron"*. [17] That is in Qur'an. But understand that the word, "revealed", used in Qur'an means, "sent down." The Arabic word, "nazala," means, "To send down". I'm sure that has reference to the objects that fall from the sky, burn up and later they find metal. Also, lightning strikes and burns the ore, making metals. I'm sure it has reference to that. The Qur'an is not talking about something that does not exist. The Qur'an is talking about what happened on earth and what exists in the life of mankind. It is not talking about something that did not happen in the life of mankind.

Spiritual and Scientific Messages

The Qur'an is a scientific message and the Bible is, too. These are not only spiritual messages. They are scientific messages and that should turn our minds on to knowledge and science to show us what is happening, today. These messages only came to those who searched, who had an orientation in their minds like scientists have. Their orientation was to search and study and to try to verify things, to try to find the truth. They were truth seekers. That is who they were. The Bible says, *"Know you the truth and the truth shall make you free"*.[18] So that means they were searching for the truth and the Qur'an says, *"The truth comes and knocks the brains out of falsehood"*.[19] They were truth seekers and it should be understood that the Prophets and Messengers of G_d were really students.

So, a rebirth came with the Qur'an and it gave the world a rebirth; a rebirth of scientific orientation in their brains, in their thinking. The Qur'an gave them a rebirth. They had lost that. The world was in darkness when Muhammed came. Even

Christianity was in ignorance and their publics suffered and were oppressed. Their females could not seek education. Their common males were made slaves, treated like animals. They did not care what color or race you were. They were treated like animals because they thought the divine spark, what they had of Scripture, could only come to certain people. If you were not blessed with that you did not deserve to be treated like a human being. You deserved to be treated like an animal.

Far From the Way of Jesus Christ

It was believed that there were two levels for human life; one in the mortal body, the flesh. That's the animal. The other one was believed to be in the spirit that G_d gives by inspiration, by way of Scripture. But, they had gone astray from the way Jesus taught. They were not with the way he taught. They believed that they should be all spiritual while at the same time rule the material world and keep it under them. That was the age or era of the Gnostics. The Gnostics were Christians but they were far from the way of Jesus Christ when G_d brought Muhammed and gave him to the world with the Qur'an. Because of Muhammed they came back to Christ's way. It was Muhammed coming with the Qur'an that brought science back to the scientific-minded people and who helped them to get back to the direction that Jesus Christ gave them.

8

No Unjust Suffering

"Whatever misfortune happens to you is because of the things your hands have wrought, and for many of them He grants forgiveness. Nor can you frustrate (aught), (fleeing) through the earth; nor have you besides G_d any one to protect or to help".[20]

The above verses from the Qur'an are addressing those who are always complaining against G_d. It is not addressing believers. It is addressing those who always want to blame G_d for their bad situation; those who are always complaining and blaming G_d for their problems. They are the people who have messed up life for everybody else. In plain language, or straight to the point, they are getting punished. They are being punished for their deeds. That's what it is saying.

These are wrong doers. It's talking about wrong doers, those who always want to say G_d is an unjust G_d; that if there is a G_d, then this world is a mess and it's His fault. There are college professors who say that and try to break the faith in others, especially in their students. They say, "Do you believe in G_d? How can you believe in G_d with all of this misery and suffering? Mother Nature is cruel". That's what they say.

They didn't just begin to do that. They did it in ancient times, in the time of the Prophets. So these verses from Qur'an are addressing those who want to say, "Look how life is made so miserable. We're making life better. We're the ones who come to the sick and help the sick. We're cleaning up this mess for that G_d you believe in"! They blame Mother Nature, too. They believe Mother Nature is cruel. So that mind is the one that is being addressed when it says, *"Whatever you are suffering, your own deeds have brought it about".*[21]

My understanding is that no one suffers unjustly. This is philosophical also, by insight. I myself suffer. Sometimes I can hardly sleep, getting up every twenty or thirty minutes. I have to get up and go to the washroom, etc. But I know that I have type II diabetes and should not eat too much sugar. So, who's sending me to the washroom? I'm responsible for sending me to the washroom. Now, that's a simple case, a simple situation.

What Sin Did the Child Commit?

But, what about a child who's born with a physical defect? What sin did the child commit? He committed no sin, but he has a physical defect. Now, I see it two ways. The explanation is given from two different perspectives, or two different views. In one view the explanation is (and I do believe this with all my heart, mind and soul) if the parents would live better we wouldn't have these defects. We inherit these defects from parents who abuse the life and the abuse doesn't always have to be physical because sometimes mental abuse is worse on the life than physical abuse. If we carry bad thoughts all of the time they can affect us physically and it does affect people, physically. They say you can be young and worry can turn your hair gray. So that's evidence right there that the condition inside can affect the condition outside.

I believe, like many good Christians, that we should not have had all these diseases like syphilis, cancer, etc. If we had kept a good spirit, a good nature and had been clean and correct inside and outside, we wouldn't have these problems. I don't believe we would have them. But, as I said, this is deep and philosophical.

So, I believe if we can get back to our original purity and innocence, it will overcome all of these diseases. They say people who get close to G_d and have good thoughts about themselves and others suffer little or no worry and little or no disease.

After I came to that conclusion I said to myself, "Well, yes, the way they live messes up the environment and punishes life, causes us to have diseases, defective births and everything". I was convinced of this and that was clear in my mind. But, now, here is an innocent child starting out in life. Why should that fall upon the generations, especially innocent babies? Then, I said, "G_d's plan goes before and beyond everything that can happen in His creation, so why this innocent baby?" G_d knows who to put a burden on. It (Qur'an) didn't say He doesn't burden. It just says He doesn't burden any soul beyond its capacity.[22] What does that mean? It means when you reach your capacity you'll die and that's G_d's Mercy, too. He takes the pain away. He takes you out of the pain, away from the pain. That's His Mercy. So, He knows the life and He knows how much to burden it or when to leave it free of burden. If He burdens it, that's His decision. He knows best and if G_d burdens you and you didn't earn punishment your burden is a blessing.

The Suffering Savior

I have more misery now than I have ever had in my life, physical misery, and I'm more qualified to advance G_d's cause than I have ever been in my life. So what's the purpose of this pain? It's to keep my conscious aware of my Lord, because we naturally turn to Him when we get pain. I keep Him on my mind now and I keep a little pain in the body; a sign of the Suffering Savior. He suffered but this kept his mind on his G_d.

You know the doctor says, "Well, I can make you better now. I can get you in better shape, but it's going to be a little painful. If you don't mind the pain, you can anticipate it getting a little better". So it is with our Lord. Sure, it can be painful, but we should believe, firstly, that G_d would not permit a servant of His to carry pain, to be in misery, if it wasn't for that servant's benefit. Down the road we will get the reward. He's assisting our soul's effort. He's assisting our soul in its effort to please G_d and achieve what G_d wants. So He is assisting it and sometimes He assists it by making the body miserable.

I used to say, "Let me get out of here so I can be with my G_d. There's too much confusion going on in this house". But now, there is nothing they can do in the house to take my mind off of my G_d. No, He's on my mind all of the time and I do know pain helps. The body's suffering helps.

Authority to Inflict Pain Belongs to G_d

However, I don't believe in inflicting pain upon myself. That would be a sin. We're not to inflict pain upon ourselves, like we're not to commit suicide or take our own lives. If we do that we are taking from G_d an authority that belongs only to Him. It's His authority to give or to take life. It belongs only to Him and if I inflict pain or misery upon my mind that's a great sin. So I do what I can to keep my body healthy and free of disease and pain because that's my responsibility. And I understand the way of G_d, too. That's His body. He created it. If He wants to punish it, He can and I am most happy with Him doing that.

This is also applicable on the group or community level. What applies to a person applies to a community and vice versa, because G_d says in Qur'an, *"Your death and your resurrection are as one soul"*.[23] So, whatever afflicts one soul also afflicts the community and whatever delivers one soul also delivers the community.

G_d also says in Qur'an, *"Your own self, your children and your possessions are only trials"*.[24] If you pass the test by remaining steadfast in faith, then G_d is going to reward you many times more than you have suffered. That goes for an individual and for a group or community, because when He puts you to trial or tests you, and you pass the test, you expect a reward and He rewards many times over. This life is easy to bear if we know G_d's love, as the Scripture says. If we know G_d's love the life is easy to carry.

Another Reality for the Soul

I believe that for some souls it is G_d's Will that they have no experience in this life at all and He takes them, immediately, to another life, another reality. I do believe that there's another reality that none of us know and sometimes G_d decides that a particular birth should not be for this world. So, He takes it, denies its entrance into this world and it goes straight to a higher world. But who knows why? Maybe G_d knows that if it is born in this world it's going to be an innocent child and it is going to suffer more misery than it can bear. It may be that G_d knows that if that child is born into this world that child is not going to have an opportunity to develop and have a good life, or not even have an opportunity to compete in a world like this. So He sends it on to another world and I sincerely believe it's a higher world, a higher reality than ours.

There is something else I believe and it is supported by the Qur'an. You know, you hear about what is called, a bad seed. G_d denies some people children, period, and there may be many reasons for denying them children. A few persons that I know that haven't given birth to children, knowing them and observing them over all these years that I have known them, oh, it's a mercy to the human seed that they didn't have children. Now, that's what I can see. My insight is very limited, but that I can see. So how do we know? With the still born, G_d may be saying, "I'm going to punish you by letting you see what has formed in your life because of your relationship with this person. But you'll just see it. You'll never have it". And then G_d sends it on to some other place. That's a punishment.

I know a person who said of her children, "I regret that I had either one of you. I wish that I had flushed you down the toilet!" Do you hear that? That's her exact words. "I regret that I had any one of you! I wish that I had flushed you down the toilet!" Consequently, she had two still births.

Lastly, life is too complicated for us to understand with our sadness, hurt and whatever. But we should give it to G_d and believe in G_d; that He is a good G_d. He's a just G_d. He's a merciful G_d. He's a loving G_d. We would then know that whatever He does is for our good.

I know that whatever we want to do of good, if we are really serious about it, we can do it. If we want to make billions of dollars for a good cause, G_d is with us and all we have to do is act. He's going to make the way for us and He is going to make the act productive. Even if we can't do it, or we reach our limitations, He'll take over from there. Now, we're not going to be foolish and put G_d to the test. We shouldn't do that, not knowingly. But, I know we don't have to be afraid or hesitant. We don't have to fear making progress. Make the effort and G_d is going to be with us, always.

9

Nothing Given Without Struggle

G_d in the Qur'an speaks of two highways.[25] One is called, the mustaqeem, the steep highway. You go up and it is steep, difficult to climb. The other is called the sabeelillah, or the horizontal path or highway. You are supposed to be on the seraatal mustaqeem, the upright path, and you are to follow the sabeelillah, which means G_d's path for you living your life out on this earth, interacting with relatives and other people, other interests. So the path goes straight up and it goes horizontal. It is very difficult to keep one's life straight up, steep, like a mountain because the incline is so steep going straight up. This is the pathway of personal life and virtues and it is very difficult. The one in the world, the horizontal path, is difficult, too. But if you manage the first one it makes the second easy or easier.

Nothing Without Struggle

Nothing is given without struggle. G_d says in Qur'an that He made the human being to be put into toil and struggle, difficulties.[26] "Kabad", is the word for this toil and struggle in the Qur'an. Nothing is going to come easy. It is a test. The learned leaders in Al-Islam they all will tell you that right away. If you accept them as your teacher, the first thing they're going to impress upon you is to understand that life is a test. It is a trial and involves suffering. It's going to be unimaginably hard for you. G_d will just let things come against you and it will be unimaginably difficult and hard for you. You will want to cry and give up. As G_d says in Scripture, the believers were tested so much until they were ready to just cry, break down and give up saying, *"When (will come) the help of G_d?"* [27]

However, if you remain steadfast, you get a measure of blessing and rewards equal to what you suffered and then G_d adds to this many times over. But He won't stop there. G_d says in the Qur'an He gives without counting.[28] We know it is not law. He doesn't read a law book to say, "How much should I give Wallace?" or, "How much should I give Sister Maryam?" His Will and Spirit just throw so much out to you that you have more than you can manage, more than you ever could imagine.

G_d will reward you very generously without counting. He says in Qur'an He gives without counting. That is to tell us, "You made a thousand dollars more this month than you thought you were going to make, but some poor sister, or brother needs something; and you can give them everything in your wallet and you still will be alright. So why count?" That's not for G_d. That is for you to open up your heart so that you don't count all the time. You know you have plenty. Don't count, just give it to them.

The tree is a parable of human establishment. The Scripture mentions an established tree firmly placed or fixed in the earth with its roots holding to the ground, holding inside the earth. Its life is supported by the strong base that it has in the ground and it grows up perpendicular. It grows up not leaning to the right, not leaning to the left, not leaning back, and not leaning forward. It grows straight up.[29]

What does that straight up growth do for the human spirit, human life, the soul and everything? It takes the burden off of the life. By balancing, the burden is taken off of the life. You walk about and you're not conscious of your weight. That is the balance G_d created to help you stand upright and the weight is equally distributed, like the tree.

People Put Themselves into Hell and Suffering

People allow themselves to be put into hell and suffering with their own hands, with their own minds. With their own sensitivities and spirit they put themselves in a hell. A baby would scream and cry until a change is made before it would live like some adults. When you were a baby you didn't like filth. You cried to have mommy or somebody to come and change your wet diaper, come and take the feces off of you and wash you up. Some babies say, "No, you are not through. You are not going to leave my skin burning just wiping me up with some tissue paper and putting a new diaper on me. I need to go to the water. Wash my bottom". And they will keep hollering and screaming until you do it, because G_d didn't create human life to love filth and misery. However, when corruption takes over, suggestions are made from high up for you to do just as you please. Nobody should be telling you what to do. You should do whatever you please. If you want to walk around in the nude and show yourself off to the public that is your business, etc.

Let's get back to life of the tree as a parable of human establishment. As the sap rises the conditions come again for that life to live, to grow, bloom and blossom. The sap starts rising and the sap is the life force of the tree. It is the life force. It is the life energy and it begins to rise. Where was it? It left the body and went down into the ground. Do you see how beautifully the tree or plant life resembles in their nature the life of the human family and community? So, when we look dead the life is not gone. We say, "I can't reach my child anymore. They don't hear me. They don't see me. I can't reach them. The world has them."

Where Thinking Not Corrupt

In reality, they are like that tree that has dropped all of its beauty and life that you got acquainted with and loved. Now to you it is looking like a tree skeleton. But G_d's Word, Revelation, teaches us that that tree can bloom, again. All it needs is the right circumstances for its environment. G_d put human life, originally, or for the first time, in a situation called the Garden of Paradise and you maybe should ask, "Where is that Garden of Paradise? Where is that heaven that G_d put our first life in?" It is where thinking is not corrupt. It is where people still care about one another. It is where intelligence is growing, not selfishly, not for that compulsive ego, but for the warm heartbeat of a brother in the family of mankind. It is where there is a brother who wants to reach out to his suffering neighbor, or who cares about human life in Africa, human life in Iraq, or human life in Palestine, etc.

If you're going to be the true human being you have to be open-minded for goodness sake, not closed-minded to hide from justice and fair dealings. You have to be big-hearted to receive everybody on this planet earth who is suffering into your heart and care about them; not that you should reject your own at home. No, charity starts at home and spreads abroad as explained in both the book of the Christians and the book of the Muslims. Charity begins at home but it should not stop there. If you still have charity to share you should give a little bit to the home and a little bit to the crying life outside of your home. Then, G_d will be with us and G_d will keep us.

G_d Created Us for Struggle

Don't ever fear. G_d says it is the Satan who wants to frighten us and make us afraid, fearing that we're going to die poor or in poverty. And it is Satan, his imps and sympathizers, who want us to believe that G_d Himself is impoverished; that mankind is enriching his world by himself, because of his own mind or intelligence and efforts; that G_d is not doing anything.[30]

G_d created us for struggle. Some of us think we're going to have everything on a bed of roses. No, if somebody doesn't take those roses and cut off their stems, a bed of roses can be awfully painful, because they have sharp thorns. That's a lesson to us too. Here is a beautiful, delicate, tender rose, but look at how it had to rise above the thorns. It is not under the thorns but above the thorns. It had to grow and survive the passage of the thorns to crown itself saying, "I have become victorious. I am victorious over hard heartedness, cruelty, and defiance." You see the rose invites the lover while the thorns defy the lover saying, "Get back! Stay back!" However, the rose has ascended above that and it crowns itself saying, "I'm better than you. I'm higher than you. I deserve to be above you. I am beauty and I invite the lover."

Going Where G_d Wants Us to Go

So life is a challenge and we have to face the challenge. That means accepting that life is a challenge and then dealing with it knowing that we have already been equipped by our very human makeup to surmount it, to beat it, to get it out of our way if it is in the way of us going where G_d wants us to go. Nothing can stay in our way if we are determined to go where G_d wants us to go. We are creatures of struggle. G_d says to us in Scripture He has created us for struggle and struggle means work. G_d says if you work, your work will bring you to a state of ease. If you want comfort, relief from hardship, then work hard.

This is the principle that we need. This is the disposition we need towards challenges, difficulties, opposition, pain and suffering from obstacles in our way. We need a spirit to rise up and go out singing and dancing to meet the challenge. Don't go out looking sad like you're defeated already. Go like some of those fighters in the boxing ring. They come in the ring and they make their opponent wonder, "Is this guy happy to come in here to fight me?" That's the way we should be going into the world of work. When you get there and the man rings the bell to start the work, you should go at it as seriously as those fighters go at it.

Miracles When You Obey G_d

G_d has made us for production. Those who victimize themselves, who think they are victims, are going to be victims in life, permanently. They aren't going to ever be invited to share in the wealth and resources of the world. That kind of person cannot become productive. The person that will become productive is the person who rises up to the challenges and says, "Hey, I'm not going to accept that this is in my way. I know I'm entitled to this honor, to this dignity, to this self-respect and it's bigger than just self-respect. It is community respect. My people are entitled to community respect, so I'm not going to be satisfied with my community being neglected like this. I'm going to rise up and get this problem solved." Be determined to do it and you will see G_d with you and miracles will begin to happen.

We're living now in a time when it is very difficult for people to stick with the best life that they have. Too many things are taking the attention away from your own good life and from your ability to keep it good and realize progress for it. It is believed that our existence as human beings began in heaven and then we were awakened in the earth. It is also believed that we were put in a situation, in this earthly existence, to challenge us, to make it difficult for us to keep the good life or to realize the growth of that good life in an environment that challenges it.

We are challenged like a plant or a tree is challenged. Don't think human life is the only life that is challenged. Some plants can't grow in rocky places. Some have to even send their roots down through the small cracks and crevices of cement or rock to survive. When you really think, philosophically, human life is challenged by obstructions, things that are in the way of living and keeping the good life. When you consider those things that are in the way, you come to understand that really human life is put in conditions and circumstances that hold it back in order for it to develop its muscles and not just physical muscles. It is to develop its mental muscles, its intelligence muscles and its moral muscles, to advance the development of its muscles more.

One who wants to be physically free must accept to have to work against physical forces. The weight lifter has to work against the bar bell with weights on it and he has to try to manage to push that weight up, or to pick it up until he is able to do it, or able to do more of that kind of physical work. Also, the person who learns a skill on a job, or is given difficult work to do for pay, the more he does it the more he develops strength, muscles and skills.

Life with No Difficulty No Life

So this world is not easy, but don't say it is not good. You can't tell a fighter that punching the bag is not good, skipping the rope is not good, boxing and training for a fight and getting hit to be in shape is not good. This is life. Human life is the same.

Anyone who wants life with no difficulty, life with no challenge, is really not living. A real man wants to be challenged. A real woman doesn't want a man who wants to do nothing. She doesn't want a man who wants to be more feminine than she is. She doesn't want a man who will watch her carrying the weights around, taking garbage out to the garbage collector, digging in the yard, raking the leaves and he sits around looking like he has no work. She does not want that kind of man. She wants a man who wants to rise up and be about something worthwhile. That's human life.

Come Back to Where G_d Intended

A sign is seen in the fact that certain members of our families may be taking the wrong course in their life and don't want to listen to us. As a result they are experiencing and suffering the pain and difficulties of this secular world causing us to wonder how we can help them. The only way we can help them is to call them to get on the Ark with us. But if they won't get on the Ark with us we can't hold up the sailing. We have got to load up, keep moving and realize that we don't have the power to save them all. Actually, we don't have the power to save any of them. Those who are to be saved will join us and come with us and those who are not will be left in the waters of this world. But don't think they are totally lost in the water. They'll drown but there is coming a time when even those who drowned will have a chance to be resuscitated.

They might not follow us, but if they hold on to G_d they can have a new life, again. Nothing is ever lost. It just appears that way. Eventually, one day, everyone has to come back to where G_d intended for all of us to be.

Scripture says G_d does not want for us hardship, but He wants for us to be purified.[31] Now, isn't that a loving G_d? He knows when we get up early in the morning it is hard on the body. The human body can't think. The body can only respond, it can't think. If it could think, it would get up with us so happy. We would feel so good in the morning. But it can't think so we have to think for it. It's going to be saying, "Hey, I don't want to get up". And G_d knows it's going to be hard on us so G_d says He does not want for us hardship, but He wants that we be purified.

Better Fitness for Whole Life

When we meet the challenge, when we accept hard things that are in the way, when we accept to do that hard thing, it makes us stronger to do even more difficult and trying things. G_d really is so wise that even the pain and difficulty that He permits us to experience is training so that we will have better "fitness" for the whole life and the road ahead. So actually the suffering, pain and difficulty we experience are a "fitness" program and what athlete dreads his fitness program? He goes into it with a good spirit. He loves it. It hurts, it pains, it challenges, he suffers, but he loves it.

So let us have faith and let us get our life together. Praises be to G_d. We thank Him and we know that He is greater than anything imaginable. G_d is our Savior and our salvation. He never runs out of love and mercy for suffering humanity and He is delivering us all of the time, even if we don't know.

Notes

Introduction

1. *"O ye who believe! When ye prepare for prayer, wash your faces and your hands (and arms) to the elbows; rub your heads (with water); and (wash) your feet to the ankles. If ye are in a state of ceremonial impurity, bathe your whole body. But if ye are ill, or on a journey, or one of you cometh from offices of nature, or ye have been in contact with women, and ye find no water, then take for yourselves clean sands or earth, and rub therewith your faces and hands. G_d doth not wish to place you in a difficulty, but to make you clean, and to complete His favour to you, that ye may be grateful."* Holy Qur'an, 5:6, translated from Arabic into English by Abdullah Yusuf Ali, Tahrike Tarsile Qur'an, Inc. Elmhurst, N.Y., 2012.

Chapter 1

2. **Microcosm:** 1. a little world: figuratively used for man, as an epitome of the universe, or great world. 2. a community, village, etc. regarded as a miniature or epitome of the world. *Webster's New Twentieth Century Dictionary of the English Language Unabridged*, The World Publishing Company, Cleveland & New York, 1966.
3. **Macrocosm:** the great world, the universe, or the visible system of worlds; opposed to *microcosm. Webster's New Twentieth Century Dictionary of the English Language Unabridged*, The World Publishing Company, Cleveland & New York, 1966.

Chapter 2

4. *"It is not righteousness that ye turn your faces towards East or West; but it is righteousness to believe in G_d and the Last day, and the Angels, and the Book, and the Messengers; to spend of your substance, out of love for Him, for your kin, for orphans, for the needy, for the wayfarer, for those who ask, and for the ransom of slaves; to be steadfast in prayer, and practice regular charity; to fulfil the contracts which ye have made; and to be firm and patient,*

in pain (or suffering) and adversity, and throughout all periods of panic. Such are the people of truth, the G_d-fearing." Holy Qur'an, 2:177, translated from Arabic into English by Abdullah Yusuf Ali, Tahrike Tarsile Qur'an, Inc. Elmhurst, N.Y., 2012.

Chapter 3

5. *"This is an admonition: whosoever will, let him take a (straight) Path to his Lord. But ye will not, except as G_d wills; for G_d is full of Knowledge and Wisdom." Holy Qur'an,* 76: 29-30, translated from Arabic into English by Abdullah Yusuf Ali, Tahrike Tarsile Qur'an, Inc. Elmhurst, N.Y., 2012.

Chapter 4

6. Ibid., 7:155.
7. *"And Moses chose seventy of his people for Our place of meeting: when they were seized with violent quaking, he prayed: 'O my Lord! If it had been Thy Will Thou couldst have destroyed, long before, both them and me: wouldst Thou destroy us for the deeds of the foolish ones among us? This is no more than Thy trial: by it Thou causest whom Thou wilt to stray and Thou leadest whom Thou wilt into the right path. Thou art our Protecting (Friend): so forgive us and give us thy mercy; for Thou art the best of those who forgive'." Holy Qur'an* 7:155, translated from Arabic into English by Abdullah Yusuf Ali, Tahrike Tarsile Qur'an, Inc. Elmhurst, N.Y., 2012.
8. Ibid., 7:156.

Chapter 5

9. Ibid., 3:193
10. *New Revised Standard Version Bible*, Matthew, 10:14, Thomas Nelson Publishers, Nashville, 1989.
11. Ibid., Numbers, 22:22-35.
12. *The Life of Muhammad*, Muhammad Husayn Haykal, translated from the 8th Edition by Isma'il Ragi A. Al Faruqi, North American Trust Publications, 1976, p. 91.

Chapter 6

13. Ibid, pp. 58-59.
14. *Holy Qur'an*, op. cit., 40:57.
15. Ibid., 30:30

Chapter 7

16. Ibid., 57:28.
17. Ibid., 57:25.
18. *New Revised Standard Version Bible*, op. cit., John, 8:32.
19. **Holy Qur'an**, op. cit., 21:18.

Chapter 8

20. Ibid., 42:30-1.
21. Ibid., 6:70.
22. *"On no soul doth G_d place a burden greater than it can bear. It gets every good that it earns, and it suffers every ill that it earns..."* Holy *Qur'an,* 2:286, translated from Arabic into English by Abdullah Yusuf Ali, Tahrike Tarsile Qur'an, Inc. Elmhurst, N.Y., 2012.
23. Ibid., 31:28.
24. Ibid., 64:15

Chapter 9

25. Ibid., 90:8-18.
26. Ibid., 90:4.
27. Ibid., 2:214.
28. Ibid., 16:8
29. Ibid., 14:24-7.
30. Ibid., 3:181
31. Ibid., 5:6

About Imam W. Deen Mohammed

Imam W. Deen Mohammed was the son of the Honorable Elijah Mohammed, the leader of the Nation of Islam. His service for the promotion of universal human excellence is well documented as he established genuine dialogue between the national and international leaders of Christianity, Judaism and Islam. In 1975 (after being elected to succeed his father), he led perhaps the largest conversion of a religious group in American history, when he invited the members of the Nation of Islam to turn away from its separatist movement and to embrace the classical path of Islam, established by the Prophet of Islam, Muhammed Ibn Abdullah (the prayers and the peace be on him). His clear presentation of the religion of Islam merited him countless awards and acknowledgments. A resume of Imam W. Deen Mohammed's work and accomplishments is outlined below:

Contributions to Understanding and Cooperation between Faith Communities

➤ In 1988 he represented American Muslims at the World Parliament of Religious Leaders' meeting for "Survival of the Earth and Its Environment" in Oxford, England. Later that year, he was selected to represent American Muslims in the symbolic signing of the First Amendment Charter for Religious Freedom in Williamsburg, Virginia.

➤ In December 1994, one of America's oldest and most respected schools of theology, the Hartford Seminary, saluted Imam W. Deen Mohammed for his trailblazing work in improving Muslim, Christian, and Jewish relations with the distinguished "Cup of Compassion Award".

➤ In 1995 Imam Mohammed was selected as an International President for the World Conference on Religion and Peace. In March he addressed its governing board meeting in Copenhagen, Denmark, with a message on social development and the aspirations and responsibilities of the common person in society.

➤ On March 25, 1995, in Glencoe, Illinois, he delivered a keynote address at an historic Muslim-Jewish Convocation, along with Rabbi Alexander M. Schindler, President of the Union of American Hebrew Congregations and head of the synagogue movement of Reform Judaism in the U.S. and Canada. This represented the first public dialogue between the top U.S. leaders of Islam and Reform Judaism.

➤ On October 2, 1996, He visited with the leader of the Catholic faith, His Holiness Pope John Paul II and participated in substantive dialogue with other Vatican officials at the Vatican in Italy.

➤ On November 20, 1996, in support of the peacemaking and human rights efforts of Most Reverend Samuel Ruiz Garcia, Bishop of San Cristobal de las Casas (Chiapas), Mexico, he traveled to Chiapas as a member of The Peace Council. Other well-known members of The Peace Council are H. H. Tenzin Gyatso, 14th Dalai Lama, Most Rev. Desmond M. Tutu, former Archbishop of Cape Town, South Africa, Samdech Preah Maha Ghosananda, supreme leader of Cambodian Buddhism and Rabbi Levi Weiman-Kelman, president of Rabbis for Peace.

- In 1997 Imam W. Deen Mohammed, was presented with the, "Luminosa Award", from the Worldwide Focolare Movement, headed by Ms. Chiara Lubich, for his work in promoting dialogue and peace between worldwide religious groups.

- In June 1998, Imam W. Deen Mohammed and a delegation of more than 40 members represented the Muslims of the United States at a Congress of the Muslim Friends of the Focolare at Castelgondolfo, Italy (outside of Rome). This fourth worldwide meeting of the Focolare and its Muslim associates included Muslims from Turkey, Algeria, Libya, Egypt, Malaysia, Indonesia, The Netherlands, South America, Africa, etc., and afforded an opportunity for participants to explore new ways for Muslims and Christians (especially members of Focolare) to work together for world peace. Cardinal Frances Arinze, the head of the Vatican's Pontifical Council for Inter-religious Affairs was in attendance and made a presentation to the congress as did Chiara Lubich, leader of the Focolare and Imam W. Deen Mohammed.

- In October 1999 Imam W. Deen Mohammed was invited to speak at an Interreligious Assembly coordinated by the Pope John Paul II at the Vatican. On the final day of the assembly, attended by more than 225 international religious leaders of all faiths, Imam Mohammed addressed an assembly of more than 100,000 in St. Peters Square, along with Pope John Paul II and five other international religious leaders.

Contributions to Community Improvement

- In May 1995, the Forbes Forum officials invited Imam

W. Deen Mohammed to address their prestigious annual conference on the topic "How to Save Our Youth".

> In February 1995, coordinators of the first, "Acts of Kindness Week" (which inspired similar events in major cities throughout America) in Dallas, Texas, invited the legendary Rosa Parks, Martin Luther King III, and Imam W. Deen Mohammed to be honorary chairpersons.

> In 1996, Imam W. Deen Mohammed established the Collective Purchasing Conference (CPC), a limited liability company designed to allow small business people the opportunity to compete in the larger business market by using the power of collective purchasing.

> On May 21-26, 1998, he was invited to travel to Bangladesh to meet with Bankers and Businessmen of Bangladesh to explore business opportunities for the Collective Purchasing Conference.

Projection of an Accurate Image of Al-Islam

> In 1990 following the invasion of Kuwait and at the invitation of the ruler of Saudi Arabia, King Fahd Bin Abdulaziz Imam W. Deen Mohammed led a delegation of Muslim leaders, scholars, and educators to Saudi Arabia where he addressed the Islamic Conference on the Persian Gulf Conflict, as the leader of Muslims in America. Imam Mohammed also served in a consultative role in the discussion of the concerns of Muslims over the Gulf War.

> On February 6, 1992, Imam W. Deen Mohammed became the first Islamic representative to deliver an invocation on the floor of the United States Senate.

> In March 1992, in Georgia, the state of his father's birth,

he delivered to a standing ovation of elected officials the first address by a Muslim leader on the floor of the Georgia State Legislature.

➢ On September 10, 1992, he was cited for exemplary work in the religion of Islam by Egypt's President, Hosni Mubarak, and was presented with the country's highest and most distinguished religious honor, "The Gold Medal of Recognition."

➢ On December 7, 1993, he delivered a historic address, "Islam and Universal Values: How Muslims Are to Contribute to World Peace," at the Los Angeles World Affairs Council.

➢ In October 1994, the leader of an estimated 60 million Muslims of Uzebekistan, Mufti Abdullah Mukhtar, visited the United States for the first time. His only public meeting and dialogue was with Imam W. Deen Mohammed at Masjid Bilal in Cleveland, Ohio.

➢ In December 1995, he led a delegation of members of the Muslim American Society to Saudi Arabia to participate in talks with Saudi Arabian education officials, as a guest of the ruler of Saudi Arabia, King Fahd Ibn Abdulaziz.

➢ In the fall, 1996, he was invited by President Hosni Mubarak to return to Egypt to address the Supreme Council of Affairs in Cairo on the theme: "Islam and the Future of Dialogue between Civilizations."

➢ In December 1996, Imam Mohammed, along with a small delegation of American Muslims, visited Jerusalem, the West Bank and Gaza, to take part in talks with the leader of the Palestinian people, President Yassir Arafat, and other Palestinian leaders.

➢ On January 6, 1997, Imam W. Deen Mohammed was

invited by President Bill Clinton to the White House to attend the First Annual Ecumenical Breakfast. On
➢ January 20, 1997, Imam Mohammed read from the Muslim holy book, the Qur'an, at the Presidential Inauguration Day National Prayer Service.

Publications

Mohammed Speaks, WDM Publications, 1999
Focus on Al-Islam, Zakat Publications
Al-Islam, Unity and Leadership, The Sense Maker, 1992
Islam's Climate for Business Success, The Sense Maker, 1995
An African American Genesis, Progressions Publishing Co., 1986
As the Light Shineth From the East, W. D. Mohammed Publishing Co.
Religion on the Line, W. D. Muhammad Publishing Co., 1983
Challenges that Face Man Today, W. D. Mohammed Publishing Co., 1985
Imam W. Deen Mohammed Speaks from Harlem, N.Y., W. D. Muhammed Publishing Co., 1985
Progressions Magazine, Progressions Publishing Co., circa 1980

Statements from Imam W. Deen Mohammed

I thank you, not as a Muslim in the sense that the world sees Muslims, nor as a Christian, or a Jew, or as a member of any religious denomination. We all have so much in common that is interchangeable and inter-related that I find it better to ignore religious labels and to deal only with a person's true beliefs.

Therefore, I join you as one who believes in an Almighty Creator of Heaven and Earth, for all of us have the right to speak and feel comfortable among people anywhere on earth. We are all one creation and our belief in One Creator unites us in spite of artificial divisions of race, color and natural origin. We are united by the most powerful bond of all-our common human origin. The real issues that concern us and affect our social and economic destiny and the destiny of our children's children are vital to all and are more profound than any ideological differences that we may have.

Our enemy is not the free world, or the Communist world, nor Christianity, Judaism, or any other religion. Our enemy is ignorance, racism, oppression, greed, and corruption. To eliminate these enemies, we must establish truth, justice, opportunity and compassion for all people. I have whole-heartedly accepted this mission with the guidance of G_d. Please join me and unite to reconstruct our human lives.

****

"Where Is the Darkness and Where Is the Light?"

In this age of science and technology, more and more of us humans are accepting that the earth mothered all of us and, by and large, we humans are more good than bad. Hence, with our different colors, facial features, languages, political ideas and religions, we all have the same birthrights: We have the right to share space here and we have the right to dream of a better existence. That is to say, each member community has a right to its own plans, to the future of its own dreams.

What lights the way for each of us to dream, to plan and to work out a better future for ourselves here is a present and growing willingness among ethnic groups to tolerate each and to give equal recognition and respect to each other. The more we are moved to get acquainted with each other, to know more about what we separately live for and what we will die for, the more we grow to like what is admirable in all of us, to invite and welcome contributions of excellence from each of us, into our worlds, the brighter the future will be, for us all.

Imam W. Deen Mohammed
Utne Reader Visionfest,
New York, N.Y.
January 26, 1999

****

"Big corporations say if you have an invention you had better hurry up with it, because just like you get it somebody else is going to have it, soon. Nobody has to steal it, but what G_d gives us, blesses us with, if you don't act upon it He will wake it up in somebody else. I know that is real. But I do know the psyche of humans, of the whole of humanity on this planet earth, is like one pool of water. You touch the quiet surface with your fingers and the ripples cover the whole pool. That is the way the human psyche is. The soul is the psyche. It is just like that. It won't reach you consciously. In some it will reach them with such energy, condensed or compact energy and it will make such an impact on their soul that it will register on their mind that, "This is a psychic communication. I am receiving something by mental telepathy". They will be convinced of that. And G_d (in the Qur'an) says the earth is going to behave one day as though its Lord revealed to her. It said the earth, not Adam, not the son of man, not an individual, but the earth itself.

What does that mean? It means this earth is growing life to come to the destiny that G_d wants for all life. And when it grows to the extent that it can connect all life it is going to connect all life, eventually. It did not take a Prophet to predict that. It took a thinking man to predict that. We see this population increasing here, there, everywhere. One day we all are going to meet and we are going to connect and then the earth will have one community of human beings and that is when it is going to behave as though its Lord revealed to it; and that is now in our time. Finally, it has happened.

I wish I could spend about one thousand lifetimes with you. That is what it would take for me to share all that G_d has blessed me with...We should be about giving America, with hopes that it will reach the whole world, the best of what we have so that it becomes even a greater America for all of us and for the world".

Imam W. Deen Mohammed
February 2, 2008